Prete

MW00681378

Also by Priscila Uppal

How to Draw Blood from a Stone

Confessions of a Fertility Expert

Pretending to Die

Priscila Uppal

TORONTO

Exile Editions

2001

Text Copyright © PRISCILA UPPAL 2001
Copyright © EXILE EDITIONS LIMITED 2001

All rights reserved. The use of any part of this publication,
reproduced, transmitted in any form or by any means, electronic,
mechanical, photocopying, recording or otherwise stored in a
retrieval system, without the prior consent of the publisher is
an infringement of the copyright law.

This edition is published by Exile Editions Limited,
20 Dale Avenue, Toronto, Ontario, Canada   M4W 1K4

SALES DISTRIBUTION:
McArthur & Company
c/o Harper Collins
1995 Markham Road
Toronto, ON
M1B 5M8
toll free:
1 800 387 0117
1 800 668 5788 (fax)

Design and Composition by TIM HANNA
Composed and Typeset at MOONS OF JUPITER
Cover Photo-collage by TRACY CARBERT
Interior Photos TRACY CARBERT & TIM HANNA
Author Photo by JOHN REEVES
Author Painting MICHAEL P. CALLAGHAN
Printed and Bound by AGMV MARQUIS

The publisher wishes to acknowledge
the assistance toward publication of the Canada Council
and the Ontario Arts Council.

THE CANADA COUNCIL | LE CONSEIL DES ARTS
FOR THE ARTS | DU CANADA
SINCE 1957 | DEPUIS 1957

ONTARIO ARTS COUNCIL
CONSEIL DES ARTS DE L'ONTARIO

ISBN 1-55096-519-0

*For those who choose grief
as well as joy*

for Chris & shannon

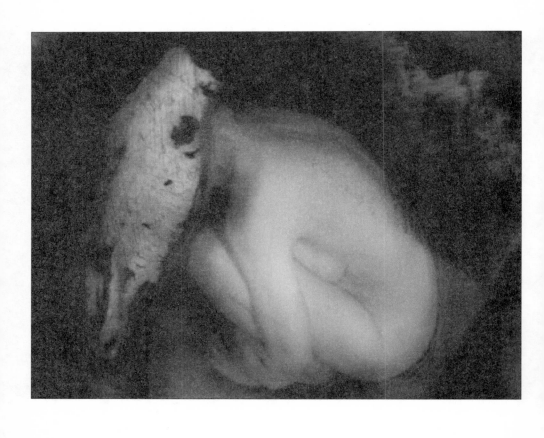

Contents

Signs of Life

Reincarnation

Purgatory

Because a Body Drowns

Pulled from the Lake

Foretelling God

Layer after layer of autumn leaves are swept away.
Something forgets us perfectly.
LEONARD COHEN

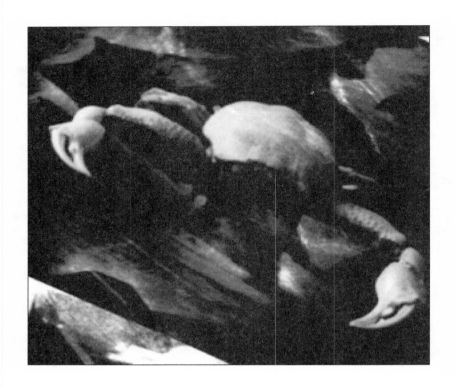

Signs of Life

Let us go.
The end of woman (or of man, I think)
Is not a book

ELIZABETH BARRETT BROWNING

Turning to Salt

It begins with a peel of wallpaper
a camera's sharp lens
and soon a curtain of eyes
replaces your clothes.

It begins with the simplest desire:
ceiling plaster melts and carpets
rip. Ants are having a field day.
Broken mirrors the least
of the year's disasters.

When my touch begins to burn
like my father's did (*one arm
asleep—the pins and needles—the other
doesn't seem to belong to me. Stand
back.*) pack the bags.

Promise me, if I am crumbling
don't look. Feel free
to grab your wife (keep clear
of dust) and storm out
of the collapsing city.

Signs of Life

The Russian lady on the corner has begun
to keep the porch light on for her son,
who moved twenty years ago.

A street party bursts spontaneously after the hockey game
and the loudest participants were cheering the losing team.

Two days ago the rose bush bloomed in spite of itself.

(I tell you this because there is a way out, out the back
of the kitchen if you jump over the drunk in the doorway
who's harmless anyway and find the extra key your ex left
under the mat hoping one day you'd follow. If you can still lift
your head and not gawk at the tower in the distance
but at the vision overhead, keep on til you feel water at
your feet; then there is time.)

An old man sells his Bible for a bag of candy.

The wheelchair, in the corner, collects dust.

My friends have filed for a mass divorce
from the past.

The spot on my clothing is not going to come out.

Stop: I tell you this because
a little girl on recess at the schoolyard
is scratching her name into the pavement until it bleeds.

Imagining a Bullet

Before the invention of guns
It was possible to kill
By shutting one eye
And aiming for the heart.

The First Sign of Fire

Wake to the smell of disaster
in your lungs
like a swift change in weather.

Grab a blanket or coat
for protection
and crawl along the floor.
Search for a light
on the other side
of the door.

Press your ear against a wall—
there is the heartbeat
of the flame

do not blame its hunger

like all newborns
it grows quickly

testing the limits.

The Tornado's Mandate

Forget you have a history, personal or otherwise.
Forget you were once a child and developed an intellect,
eccentric tastes, a love for someone.

Your mother
has abandoned you and your father's out drinking.
The landscape is empty as your arms. Like any institution
we plan to keep you to ourselves—we are your Children's Aid,
your Orthodox Church, your National Embassy—we care
little for your particular circumstances
or fears. If you hide, we will expose you.

Your home
has shattered like glass. Your sex has flown away. Your age
no longer thinks of you.

In the dark you will
be guided back to a place of no known name, a place
of rootlessness and precarious survival.

Admire:

around you stately statues have toppled. Men and women
whose dates you memorized are no longer alive. The tree
you swung from that summer has been pulverized.

This is war. Your spirit
under siege.

If you plan on living, you must be solitary. You must be wind,
rain.

Scissors Etiquette

Appear casual.

Work efficiently
and happily
and no one will suspect
you of danger.

Shine yourself once a week.

Exercise daily.

Keep out of the reach
of children.

Remember: you control
your destiny.

Hang yourself where
you can be seen.

And don't shake anyone's hand
unless you plan
to be party to a murder.

The Girl with the Left Shoe on the Right Foot

She's the one mother wishes
she never had, the one father wishes he had
beaten more often.

If Abraham

If Abraham hadn't responded to God's command
how much better the relationship with his son
might have been. No nights of discomfort
in the dark, calling out in his sleep
for good Samaritans, no more fights
at breakfast about the day
it almost happened, no more hiding
the largest and sharpest kitchen knives.

If Abraham hadn't heard another word
and done the deed, how many days before some troupe
of angered parents hunted him down, stood
on his lawn with signs and government officials
broke every unbarred window
in his home, how many years before
the smell came off his hands,
before he could eat meat again.

If Abraham was smart as the men in my neighbourhood
he would have destroyed evidence of his plans,
taken the boy no further than the basement,
and kept the fires burning until
not a soul could have recognized that body.

Inheritance

She knew he would go
spit out the wrong words, sprain an ankle
lose his hold on the things that matter.

In cold winters, they send red letters
with gold trimmings, wish him well and suggest
he cut out red meat and beer,

Fill flowerpots with red roses and white
lilies, give money to charities, display photographs
in sensible silver-plated frames.

Tell their own children fairy tales
about the time before, with
detailed arrangements for his safe-keeping,

inheritance. But the young man's wife has run away.
And O, she has her father's eyes and nose,
his temper and his brittle bones.

Sisyphus Invented the Wheel.

Years of love, erosion-love.
'It's a job,' he knows,
'this humanity.'

When Judgment came
he gave the gods
a push.

Pretending to Die

When I dug myself into the muddy sand
the waves seemed to roll
with new vigour. The sun burnt delirious
eyelids, I desperately tried but couldn't
keep closed.

Perchance there would be screams
and sirens, a frantic mob shedding tears,
a new mother to cradle my limp
flesh and strap her lips
firmly on mine.

Instead the tide washed in
bearing seaweed and popsicle sticks
a little girl stole my pail
even the sand abandoned me
while the one I loved for three full summers
stepped squarely upon my ribs
and kept on going.

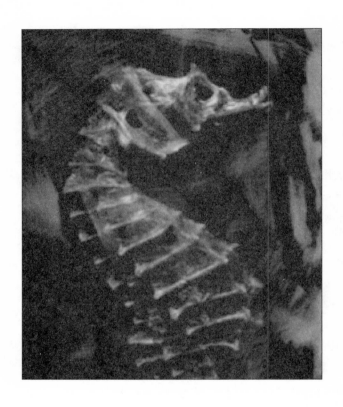

Reincarnation

I go to my knees, at length
Before the song of a bird; before
The breath of spring or fall
I am lost, before these miracles
I am nothing at all.

A.M. KLEIN

Engineering Disaster

I

The degree to which you ascribe
is proportional to your loss

if you've burned a bridge
build one

II

The math simple
it is the execution which falters

from mismatched electricity
an entire city explodes

My Ambition

I wanted to know
what it was like to be my father
so I left my country with nothing but a letter
and a scholarship that was revoked
as soon as I landed. Went to work
for an Englishman
who sold books he couldn't read.
At night paid the day's wages
for language lessons from another immigrant.

Next I took a job and worked
my way up to manager, and knew
I was doing good, found a delicate wife,
a house with a reasonable mortgage,
a pool, a couple of kids,
and the kind of attitude my family
back home would not stand for.
I had arrived.

Then I shattered my spine with a stick
spent my life tied to a chair
begging for food and water
for my wife not to leave me
for my children's love on holidays.
I could barely afford to get my glasses fixed
to see the damage
let alone send my children to college.

Now I can sympathize
with the many letters
he writes to no one in particular
and the detailed ledgers he keeps in the basement
of canned goods and the number of foreign
news correspondents on television. It's important
to keep accounts
be able to predict what you can.

Yet when he calls me in the middle of the night
with another fact or statistic,
I hang up.

I have not fled from my hatred
but despise him more
seeing through his eyes
turning my ambition
into a suspicious game of chance
and pushing my withheld love
into the arms
of strangers.

Priscila Uppal

The Third World

You used to live there
arrived on a plane
with winter behind you
told the wells needed
to be drained
and filtered
the main bridges
realigned

but it was the hunger
that startled you
wide bellies
of fear
fists filled
with seed
that refused to grow

they trusted you
to take them
out of this
to fire the land
mix ashes in your hand
bless the waters
with a wisdom handed down
from the west

it all blew by so fast

now you lie like the desert
on hospital tables
nutrients extracted
by many swift hands

with nothing more
to do than trust

your fingers
to form a steeple
in the unnerving sand

Sex with Columbus

We rode the waves in a month-long stretch
of glorious discovery. My body meeting him
like a welcome error: odd instrument of his
marking round territory.

It was supposed to be a secret between us
and the sea.

Later I heard he bragged to his buddies.
Claimed to be the first, though he wasn't.

Samson was a Narcissist

True, he was strong, but who wouldn't be
with all that mismade money in his pouch.
No pickpocket in town could have slipped
fingers between his to catch a couple of stray
coins. Delilah knew all along what that man
needed when he came to bed his balls
ready to swing. She said, *Darling, darling,
won't you trust me?*

Philomel

He said
I could spot
one in
an instant.

The beauty of
the bird alone
makes a
man tremble
like a boy.

He said
the song
is doubly
loud because
the bird
has no legs.

But she did
not come
to the park
that day.

Instead
a girl
by a fountain
caught
our eye.

I heard
that girl
was raped.
That's what
he said.

He forced
my legs
open
to search
for her wings.

Goliath

I defy you
in your strength to dwarf me.

From my father I learned law.
From my mother, honour.

I've collected pebbles
from the beaches of Normandy.

And rock
from the Berlin Wall.

Tower of stone, I will turn
your weapons against you

and split your jaw from its bone.

The Lamp

My grandmother asked for our hands
and more lamplight before she died.
We told her the pain in her joints
was just the rain, bones shifting like clouds.
She would rise in the morning and I would curl
her limp and still black hair.

Mother brought water and vegetable soup.
We spoke about cucumbers
and smashed pale tomatoes
reminding ourselves that seasons
and grandmother's coughs are routine as spooning food.

She took it with grace and silence, her eyes
on the antique silver while I polished her mouth.
She took it with a promise we would follow
her wishes to the letter: one for the house, a second
for her soul, and the third she never could say.

Her eyes fixed on the lampshade's insolence
she dropped her lip
to draw a last breath
the last breath meant for a word.

She had three wishes, Genie, and you were not one of them.

I Refuse the Gift of Reincarnation

I don't want to begin again. Life, though
not half as glorious as once imagined,
has at least come to order. Yes, I have
troubles: a drunk father, runaway mother,
a brother who insists I'm a fly on his wall,
and you may be able to fix that next time
around. And yes, my true Love disappeared
with all the money; but I've got a pre-nup
now and eat out three times a week.
There are worse disasters than these.

In my next life I might be raped, murdered,
sliced and diced and buried around this awful
city, or my skin might be the wrong colour
for the next regime. Or I might come
back a man and I'd laugh at myself all day—
probably not the path to enlightenment.

Imagine life as a butterfly, you tease. Please.
There is a score of them circling my house.
If the day is clear we collect them in jars.
If not, we watch them slam into glass.
There is not one of us now who isn't beautiful.

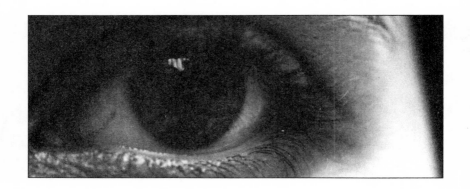

Purgatory

Let the one who's been given the work of the word accept you like an extra dark heart, and don't let him stop until he has justified the living and the dead in a single song at dawn among the grasses.

ANNE HÉBERT

The Progress of Sleep

At first I resisted you with a passion that hurt.
Jealous of night watchmen, bats and cats, winds
That wove while my eyes were closed, afraid
I'd miss the most important moment of my life. Grudgingly,
We shook hands. I lay down to the darkness.

Yet now I stay longer in your company each year,
Take naps for the sake of it, discover noon
An appropriate hour as any for rising. I see us growing
Old and comfortable, sharing a few jokes, a well-kept secret
Until the last light is drawn, where all my life can be imagined.

Meeting the Dead in Dreams

No matter how many times we've hoped
to be reunited, when at first
they appear the instinct is to flee. The dead

never look quite right—not like you remember:
two dimples where one should be,
a smudge around the eyes,
a new wool sweater in a colour
you know they'd never wear. They come

with their hands tight in fists. You swear
upon their graves that nothing is amiss.
You have carried them in your heart
as long as you could. And they open their mouths,
drop their jaws,

speechless. Then
surrounding you like a mist
is a guilt you thought you'd dealt with,
dusted clear away from the bedside table,
the kitchen cupboards, your journal. You try
to brush its urgency away but

they start to fade like streaks on glass. You want
them back harder and more sincerely
than ever.
Start to strip. Tell them to stay. Give up your clothes,
your wife,

your second chance. You've noticed how translucent

the skin, and the pigment of their eyes. They rise
like air. Seem to
ride an escalator
moving backwards...

Still afraid, you shake. Want to give
them power. A sword or a wand that would
cut you open lying there just dreaming
like that as if it were everyday, ordinary (because

it is). Want to give them the luxury of wasting
this, lie there with you as time
moves on—even if it means,
as you've suspected,
that then you too must join them.

Not Meaning to be Rude

He steps on toes and spills his wine
forgets my name because he can't
make out the haze in front of him.
Letters received go unread, unanswered,
handwriting like tracks in snow
envelopes tucked in water glasses
like napkins. He has misplaced the door keys
three times, ended up asleep on the porch,
hands planted inside dried flowerpots.

The family speaks of putting him in a home,
nurses and surgeries, the latest laser
treatments, as if he'd really lost his hearing.
He tells me, when he suspects I'm not looking,
that darkness is a place he's been before.

This month he has said goodbye
to the waters of his youth, Aegean-blue,
to the green grass of his front lawn
and the yellow impressions of autumn leaves
twig-brown centres of my aunt's eyes.
He requests they excuse his absence for now,
not meaning to be rude, party to a previous engagement,
spectacular fireworks, a splendid ovation of red.

Watering the Plants

There are days when he sleeps
so soundly I forget
he's there
secretly growing
as I tend to the plants
on his windowsill

they seem to have a pact
these plants
and my father
trading carbon for oxygen
hour upon hour

and there are moments
I almost wish
I could join them
lay my body between
and whisper I want
I want to know
what it's like
to be part vegetable

we've never been this close

finger in his mouth
pill
pushed down

until now I'd never
felt the force
of such accomplishment

water plants
while my father sleeps
in old pajamas
torn at the crotch

a plastic tube
winds down his leg
like a vine.

Raining Cats and Dogs

He went slowly,
         the nurse kept saying
we should prepare, but every
night when they let us out
we went straight to sleep
came back in the morning
         like bewildered scientists.
(How

I felt when I read that 'raining
cats and dogs'
         came from faulty pipes
and sewer systems unable to
control a storm. In the seventeenth
century their bodies littered
the streets. I couldn't
utter the expression again
         without a shudder.)
How he managed to

keep his head above water
         is a mystery;

         the rain falls
outside my apartment like
drops of insulin.

Have mercy,
I think,
let the bloated

carcass sink.

Empty Frame

The actors have gone home
to their luscious beds and odd love-making
to thoughts of children they might have
when their looks fade and work is scarce.

The party has ended. The director admitted his affair.
A lonely caterer sits holding the edge of a couch like the calves
of a man. Protesters have all paid their dues and are drinking
at the pub wondering if they've made the six o'clock news.

Banners are torn. Clothing rattles out the back
like snakes. The reels keep their mouths shut.

No one's bothered to cut the absence out. The engineer
of this dream packed his tools. Flew
straight out of the city with his passport tied to his shoes.
He drowns his sorrows (the pangs of invisibility)
on a shore in tropical Hawaii.

Priscila Uppal

Purgatory

I will meet you in purgatory with the other
outcasts, bare-faced and oblivious.
I will meet you in the elevator
stuck on the eleventh floor with a bouquet
of white roses and a silver pocket watch.

There we will discuss the effects of claustrophobia.
We will try on each other's shoes.
We will place our fingers in wire sockets
and scream like the dead.

But we will not be dead. In limbo the words
we dread to utter suspend like flashing numbers.
We will invade the space. Make ourselves room.

Come to answer for the times we sort-of sinned,
kind-of helped, perhaps guessed the right answer.

You will argue you had little to work with. Show them
stained hands. I will assert my soul was switched

at birth. The light will guide us. Eyes closed, knees broken—we will
continue to rise. Betray our disguise.
The fires, my friend, will not touch you.

The Night the Fairy Tale Made Sense

Six o'clock on a Saturday. The store
almost closed. My godmother just
settled the last account—a woman

who (she whispered later over tea in her bedroom
as she took off her blouse, her liver spots
more noticeable
nipples shifting from rose to peach)

was twenty-five and looked fifty. 'The chemo
does that sometimes, takes years off your life.'
And she hands me face cream all the way from
Hungary because there the pollution's so bad

scientists produce the most unbelievable
protection.

         She was all alone. Not rare
my godmother insists. Not many strong
enough to watch them fitted for a wig, only notice

the rough skin, patches of nothing, but
the strands that remain are soft as newborn curls—and
I wonder how she knows this, since she's never

had children. And then my godmother, wrapping
chocolate squares from a recent trip to Ireland,
says, but she's a sweet case

        still has dreams
told me her name was Rapunzel and needed
the hair so her lover could climb to her room—
that when he pulled down, she wouldn't feel a thing.

Old Men

Old men like you crumple unforgivingly
        sway in the heat
        one hand on your forehead

the other on a ledge

Old men like you breathe with long stresses
        crack knuckles on tables
        hold the phone away from your ear

When the balances are tipped
come up wanting

Old men like you make arguments with paper
        certificates and hunting licences
        old deeds and bills
        take too many pills because they are

easy to swallow

Old men like you strain before mirrors
        read with the lights off
        shake when reaching out a hand

        The deaths of children are quick but
        those of

Old men, you almost convince me,

    are slow and not
    painful though accomplished by hands
    like mine

by hands accomplished as mine.

Notes for Later

don't forget to remember the way your father's shirt used to smell
when he mowed the lawn
or how he made eggs and always broke the yolks taking them out
of the pan
or the chair he sat in reading newspapers and smoking Colt's sliding
his glasses on then off his nose
or the way he held you on his shoulders to see the animals in the parade
or how he painted your room blue when you asked
and even how he cried when you left and cried when you returned
asking why it always takes so long to get time off
or a second on the phone
and the light that still shone in his eyes when he knew you lied

At the Forks of the River

Even though they buy ice-cream
half the customers seek directions.
For the place they've heard about, a rumour
of red leaves and murmur of the Credit.

The girl next door has just found
the world of boys, campfires, and
train trestles, her teacher takes her shopping
for a graduation dress. Her father, not
bending to work beneath him, lets her
walk in leaky shoes.

Already she is like the passing cars seen from the store.
We can barely make out her face behind the glass.

When the shades are drawn, the store
closed, the frogs mate carelessly, seduced
by the sound of voices. Each call brings
them closer.

In this place there are no fathers
and the children scatter as seasons.
If you're still you can almost see yourself
erasing into a curve in the road.

The Search for Seashells

On the dirty beach where even lifeguards
Refuse to dip bare feet and blood-sucking worms
Are too tired for the chase, father said we should
Amuse ourselves searching for seashells. Even
This area of brown sand and broken glass might
Prove to be the dusty cover of something beautiful.
As he wore himself thin in the heat, his hair shedding
Into the tides, we waded with our pails and plastic
Shovels, piling dirt on either side of the safety line
Until the sun went down. The hole we dug
Proved the exact size for a small child and father
Pushed his ear against the black and swore the sound
Of the ocean underneath was the voice of someone
He could almost, almost recognize.

Orpheus

In the first days of my marriage
my only thought was to be heard

hear me sing of a love unharmed by rough winds
hear me sing of a passion untouched by rain

to lose her once I lost my audience
to lose her twice I lost my nerve

underneath her body preserved
her face formed to the tip of my tongue

I have lost track of my travels, currently
each song changes with the times

see me floating across the damp banks of your river
see me drift out of the corner of your eye

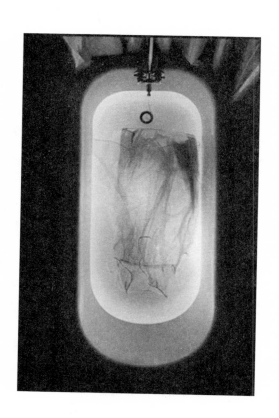

Because a Body
Drowns

Grief knocks, because it's uninvited.
Anon

Searching the Dictionary

After your death I took to reading.
Not the classics you had in mind we would enjoy
together; *Othello, A Tale of Two Cities, Madame Bovary*
or *War and Peace*. It wasn't narrative I sought (what did I care
about the intrigues of kings or bored French wives), or even poetry
(no one could convince me of beauty, prosody, terrible
transcendence). I wanted the one word that would speak you.
I ransacked the dictionary.

Nothing came close. Adjectives and adverbs were all
distraught. Words like *here*, or *there*,
quietly, gently, goodnight. Haunting me in the strangest
places, between leaves on the ground by our walkway
or the grocery line-up where hands grabbed food
demanding *cans, cartons, bottles, boxes*. But where
were you hiding?

So I delved into words that crossed between places: *merge,
blend, saturate, osmosis*. Words that broke: *crack, wedge,
distill, violate*. Words that stung: *missing, vacant, error, love*.
All were inadequate, as is the word *inadequate:* insufficient, not
capable or competent, lacking.

And I refuse to go to the Old Book, the First Dictionary.
Christ never impressed me. He was all love. He got
to come back and say *so long* properly, *see you later*
and know it would be true.

Priscila Uppal

There is no word to describe the way
I touch you and can't touch you simply sitting on a streetcar
or sipping my soup, nor the sense of disintegration
I feel every time the phone rings. No
word for how I've started to divide my friends
in terms of those I can afford to lose and those I can't.

Procession

For you, who have never been one
to insist on ceremony
we start the line-up backwards
to mourning   your casket
filled with hope   white sheets
and colour

In the silence
hands are shaken   held tightly
as if to chain you there   and we
all hope someone will produce
the appropriate gesture
(the one that will make you breathe—
stop the stiffening of your lids)

Shut down   parades
paper hearts and good luck charms
burn with your eyes and hair
while the minister pronounces
we must prepare for death, more than life:
the only part of his sermon
that makes sense
to me

Black urns   grey frost
(dust to dust)
your children hang off their uncle
like broken swings
while in your rest
you rise
      and fall
          and rise
            again.

No More Funerals

Last year and this year I wear
these shoes and this pleated skirt
as if to work. I even thought
I might need to buy a new outfit
so as not to offend anyone,
though my circle of friends
is getting smaller.

We are all tired now and can't
put up the fight. Trees hang
and stars blink. Every living
thing has bent halfway.

The earth does not tremble.
We are sinking, shrinking,
back to seeds.

I refuse to cut any more flowers.

No more, Death, take your prisoners.
In these clothes
I claim: black is the colour
of surrender.

Almost In-laws

At your kitchen table
cutting vegetables for dinner
one month since the funeral
someone innocently puts on
an album from your collection
and I recall the conversation
we were supposed to have about the time
Robert Plant blew me a kiss.
Your sister said, "Oh, you have to tell
her, she'll die. She'd just die
if she knew."

Now tea suggests tea I should have
brewed and vegetables slip
through our hands
pared clean of dirt
in the house you painted
alone, where you cooked
alone, and many are necessary
to perform the same feasts.

Light diminishes slowly in the evening
without applause or ceremony
in the air of disappearing dinner conversation
the kisses of aging rock stars
and almost in-laws drift down
like snow in remote places

remaining untouched, unanswered.

Ordering Your Death

Because we knew it was coming, we thought
we could plan. Spread you upon a table, pin
your bones to the sides, wash your arms
the same as windows, spray you with perfume.

It was going to be beautiful. Your skeleton restored
like a fine antique and when friends and family arrived
the corners of your mouth, the folds on your stomach,
could be admired in a simple state, an open house.

It was going to be beautiful. But once you were bare,
brittle and light, you lit up like newspaper.
And for the next cold year the inspectors kept saying
we put the entire neighbourhood in danger.

A Few Notes on Your Grief

at night you fold like a fan

and it's not me you reach for

you read over shoulders

push people in line

breathing has become a chore

old men and fountains amaze you

the ceiling seems far, very far

the scent of apple mocks you

fear of heights has disappeared

you find you are alone and not alone

crying is no longer an act of release

flowers have grown meaning again

Because a Body Drowns Not by an Excess of Water, But by a Lack of Air

all his grief is in his feet
in the stairwell where you used to hide and paint pictures
        of autumn trees and broken dreams
in the yard where the cicadas stretch their weary stems and swings
        sway in the push of the wind
in the shopping malls where you lined up kid by kid to make sure
        none were lost
he paces alongside store windows and display cases
        stares each mannequin in the eye

in the hospital corridors where you had your tonsils out decades ago
        and the nurses brought you cigarettes
in the train station where you took a last trip east
        claiming lost luggage and old neglected hats
in the four corners of the split highway where you could have gone to visit
        sister or mother, friend or brother
is a single sign that tells him there are five miles to go

he runs through fields of strawberries you crushed in your hand
        he runs past the bushels of blood

in the long corridors of the community centre
        between rummage sales and the gymnasium
in the parking lots
        beside florists and fruit stands

in the crammed blocks
        of the neighbourhood
in the double plots
        of the cemetery

it might be you he feels in the soles of his feet
        a slight bump, an ache
he can't locate
        a tick
he can't quite control
it might be you underneath the street in front of the house
you've never seen
making him trip

and it's the sewers he fears have taken you
moving from grate
        to grate
just out of earshot

        the water forced on
filled with dirt and rain and garbage and grief
he fears you'll drown
he fears you'll never come up again for air

Welcome the Cross

We walk amongst memorials (eyes
turned towards the ground in greed) knowing that sickness
can strike at any turn: by a television, a coffee maker,
the flick of a switch. Even the computer, my brother

says, has a virus. Nothing seems to fit
the old songs kept by my bedside for comfort.
These are no Adonises struck down by an aimless
arrow. No Hallums in pubescent health. No Thysiris.
Lycidas. No Orpheus.   In their beds

these bones dream of such glory. The hunt and the fall,
the young lovers attending services, the weeping heads
drowned in riverbeds. They welcome the cross, the stone. Fates
that are fast and glorious. Not this tunneling under the skin,
where burial goes on forever. Flower upon flower delivered
to their sides—whose short lives wilt to taunt them.

Endings

After the funeral: time to say goodbye.
Keep up appearances, hold on to flowers
and make up speeches for ritual's sake.
But ritually there is no solace for suffering.

What we leave are not wilted petals, the pictures
of doves and pillars, fresh water at the entrance.
Nor the gentle handshakes, carefully labelled plates,
or thousands of white crumpled handkerchiefs.

Sense the room: the sounds are those of anticipation.
An audience silently awaits a new reception.
If sorrow were a door it would open from the inside.
If sorrow were a match it would strike when wet.

A time of stop, over, solitary ground.
For us, like in dreams, promise me two endings.

Anniversary

November's been unseasonably kind.
Leaves strewn politely across the walkway.
The air fresh and pungent as spring.

We decide to walk. First past the house
Where you grew up, the large birch a standing
Monument of better times, branches

Worn and pinched at the chest. Next to your
Old school where the sign has changed three times
From elementary to junior high to elementary

Again. The children in their homes on Saturday,
The swings vacant like barren wombs. Onward
To the site where last year it was impossible to erect

A stone in your honour, the ground fierce and stubborn
Like our hearts, unable to let you go, cracking under
The pressure of heavy feet. Fearful we would

Harm you, dear sister, press our grief into your face,
Our hands down through your new dress and tear the box
Filled with your bones like greedy, unapologetic beggars.

The weather's been kind to us all, to your children
Grown taller and smarter, their eyes opening to the hours
Of knowing and carrying, here and there, past and

Passing. We wait for the minister and the square stone is
Measured, weighed and planted. I wanted an angel,
But mother feared wings would only taunt you

further from our home.

A Few More Notes on Your Grief

the bones in your face for years have been
turning
mother to father, the curved jaw of your brother
back
and forth
you are coming out

in the mirror you search eyelids and teeth for
her
sister you lost, so young, too young
skeleton
you dig
you are coming out

the backs of your hands, heavy and flat
wait
to enclose, touch the dream that takes shape
hopefully
you push
you are coming out

the bones in your face are making a stand
here
to be the one so young, so sister
freeze
you are coming out of stone
you are standing
breathe

Pulled from the Lake

At last the chimneys are submerged.
All the horizons point north.
The bodies, freed, float.

JOYCE CAROL OATES

The Modern Soul

Flat and shiny as the silver dollar
I keep hidden in my bedroom drawer.
Its value may decrease year by year
But I'd still bet my entire future
That some day, one dark stranger
Will fight me to the death for it.

Lament

In the interim (while I still have a voice), I must
open my mouth like a large cave and find animals
dwelling inside building shelters, foraging for food,
carving up rock into myth and resurrected rituals.

Regardless of progress, the winds still turn bitter
in November and illness comes like a thief, subtle
and wicked. The holes in my eyes have no place
to hide and the coming slaughter is a surety.

So I can do nothing but notice this crippled flower,
this twisted leg on a yellow bird. Bless the child
holding out her tired hand for change. Acknowledge
the old man throwing stones against church stairs

and wait my turn. There are laments for the lost, the weary,
the dead. Laments for those who speak for their people
and those who have no people to speak for. For the land.
For the seasons passing. For gravediggers and water diviners.

Everyone we meet, we know is temporary. So why, why,
do tribal memories insist on clinging to our skins?
Inside the wilderness of my mouth, a lion roars for the first
time today. Knows this pain he is born with is certainly ours.

A Short Sketch of Dante's Kitchen

The world is hungry, its borders
made by bread, stuffed with people
and their purses, the sound of church bells
down the street. Behind the swinging door
sadness travels by smell. And in the ovens
the yeast looms, strangely delighted in the rising fire.

Message from the Dead

On the next clear evening
as you look up at the stars, know I am coming, hurling
myself towards you at the speed
of light.

I will fail beautifully. You will not catch a glimpse
of my fatal love
or even a distant grasp of my whereabouts
yet

there are others who can
after 40 million years of wandering
the Egyptians
with treasures intact
written upon their lips in light
so harsh it burns

holding out weary arms
to the earth.
They are crying to you.
They are bleeding (music
of the spheres)

mummies
and buried women
claiming you for their own.

Do not resist
you who think it a right to be given
back the faces you've loved, held,
fed on your breast,

your aim is preposterous. Grip
the arms of your chair, this travel is longer and far
more spectacular than the first rocket
to the moon.

The orbits of the dead
are straight, targeting themselves to
your lawn chair at this very moment

coveting your blouse, your glass of scotch,
your magazine and cigarette.

Accept their presence. This is your mission too
though you'd never admit it. Your father

your mother, your dearest friend is not destined
to find you—mouth agog, millions of
lost ages light up your sky

forcing belief, an ancient belief,

down your throat.

Insects

By rumours they ride
to food and safe places. Find a father
in a dumpster, sons asleep in tree bark,
an acquaintance eating her way
through the walls.

They mate frantically for one
sweet release from searching.
One day this will end, they tell
each other. One day we will
be exposed.

Scientists speculate in the event
of nuclear war
only insects will survive:

those whose antennae are sharp
those whose eyes are multiple
those unacknowledged legislators
with many sets of hands.

The Clock

At ten minutes to midnight mice scurry
tails beating against the last of the day
and far from the clock they begin to race their way.

At nine minutes to midnight birds fly
wings stretched taught against the sky
and far from the clouds they sing.

At eight minutes to midnight flowers fold
petals spin across dirt roads
and far from the sun they wither away.

At seven minutes to midnight the counting begins…
at six and five the mountains
descend
underground.

At four minutes to midnight gods weep
glass eyes shut for sleep
and far from the clock they list the saved.

At three minutes to midnight women mourn
boys and girls forever torn
far from their homes wake from a dream.

At two minutes to midnight some find peace
if not comfort.

At one minute to midnight
suicide notes begin to be written.

Cold-Blooded Creatures

Outsiders, they mimic their surroundings.
Imitate the blues of the ocean shore.
Pound their scales into bark.
Round their bones to rocks.

In the heat of summer
their eyes grow thin and glow
like phosphorous. For years
they burrow, legs like shovels.
They see beyond the freshness
of flowers, the warm nests
of more attractive animals.

They know the insiders will come crawling
as to fortune tellers and anonymous doctors
in a time of trouble

the outer layers of their skin
burning
for a touch that freezes time.

Hospital Flowers

I

Rhododendron women
breasts clusters of showy red
purple pink white, the evergreen
foliage plucked for
safekeeping.

II

Dandelion men
heads filled with white powder
little girls shower
full hearts of promises
blow your dreams
asunder.

III

Lily children
prints on all the paintings
the smoothest flesh
formed from red soil
rest in incubators, perfect
pacified buds.

IV

Rose nurses
stuff scents and sweets
into open mouths and failing
fingers, reach out in terrible
beauty, prick their loves
with thorns.

V

Primula doctors
do not seed unless
both members are present
keep the long lines patient
for the possibility of one
miraculous flower.

In Your Sickness

It is your body, soft as an old bed,
the fleshy pillows of your fever
that make me want to deliver you like an old letter
back to a first love, aged yet tough, sitting
stout like a sandcastle on the beaches
of your lost land, waves curling and unfolding
like tides through your drowning speech.
She has perhaps forgotten you these
many years, her heart broken by stronger, crueler
men than you, her eyes the dried tunnels of travel
cursing the waters, the deep waters that bear men away.
I will say to her: here is the man I love,
you too once loved, fading now like a memory.
He is light and haze. He is specks of dust.
He has turned into a terrible mystery.
I want to bring you to her, tied in white sheets,
a welcoming ceremony in the ritualistic days
of sacrifice, days of parting. I want to hold
you in my arms the way we held our animals.
I want to flatten all your hair with my hand,
have you lick the lingering salt off my palm.

Deathbed Prayer

It is only fair now that you
who once held the wheel in your hands
and spread blankets for comfort
your eyes squinting through the darkness
for a pit-stop, a restaurant, a home in the distance
with a small light for guidance and the rear-view
mirror set like a third hand across our foreheads
to check if we were sleeping, should become a passenger
laid in white sheets and fed through our hands
some flowers to remind you of outside scenery
as it whizzes by. That your dreamy, unformed thoughts
should come through the air like hints of arrival:
a tunnel, a station, a woman you once called
to with the passion of a groom, a secret you
let escape to the water jug, washcloth, painkillers.
You, who once read maps with a fervor reserved
for the boldest travellers, a sound plan for the prepared,
must let go of such material matters, concentrate on spoon,
rest, bathroom. Let the symptoms suffer you,
dials and knobs read your direction. Leave the decisions
to your followers: when to stretch, wake, moan.
Let us keep watch. Let us keep watch. We will tell you
when you get there.

Pulled from the Lake

You were the one that broke through. And you
never forget it. Each splash you made
with your feet, a protest. *Who do You think
You are?*

It was the air you missed most. The delicious
smell of morning and the great red apples
you used to pick from the backyard. You
remember what

it was like before the cold, before the boat
took off with your wife and children, before
the long language you memorized
became defunct.

Distrust has become a veil, strong as ice.
You can hold your breath for hours.

Casualties

What shouldn't be spoken
is not the manner of death
(the disease
the accident
the crushed bones and severed
limbs
or the waxy deaths
like candle drips
that went on
and on)

among the altars and urns
the flowers and eulogies
men and women
and children hold hands
eat sandwiches in the sun while
the word *peace* surrounds
us like flies

but we don't want you to rest
in peace
we want to disturb your death
have you crash into
the church (breaking
each sacred window)
in a bright red car

make us casualties
of your passing

press your hungry mouth
against our eyes

beg us to fix this
before the newspaper men arrive

Hairless

She's been told
it's a disease

runs her fingers through
the hair
like an untamed cat

grips loose
strands in her fist
like a jaw

she can't stand the mess
the uncleanliness
of the dead

strips them bare
sends them down the stream
of her washtub

one for her father, that man
she called hunger
until he remarried

another torn
for her lover, she wore
like an old sweater
until not a thread remained

and an entire clump, gone
for the sister she never had
who would've
told her the secrets she'd
been left out of

five for the florist
who stalked her
an entire autumn

three for the trees
outside that lost
their leaves

as he stood, waiting*

four for the passenger who was never found
two for the letter that went missing
ten for the cat crushed in an engine
eight for the sky's fierce hand
one for the road

---

* There are nights the hairs return, those stubborn children of her brain, when she has dreams of hands and feet and fists and clubs and flowers crushed in medicine jars, stones pounded into eyes, fire exits, baby strollers, small men in dark costumes and women wandering through the corridors she knows she locked before going to bed.

Wind Song

I have bred this anger from your brow
the time to sweep over the earth is now

the clock has struck and birds perch
themselves on windowsills
butterfly wings hang off hooks
bleeding and hungry

forever our lives have been running
toward this end
and my eyes cannot resist your sight

I will steal you from the earth
I will steal you

The Witches of Winter

lie in cages with their beaks burnt black
as if the snow itself couldn't kill them
and their stupid friends (you know the kind)
wait at all hours for the end of the world
for the end of the world
waiting

and some children sent out for firewood
come back with necks and limbs
and warm themselves by a witch's oven
at all hours for the end of the season
for the end of the season
burning

the witches of winter disappear in dreams
falling white clusters (no two alike)
their hard black canes
beating at all hours for the end of the night
for the end of the night
waking

A Second Chance

In autumn, the season of lepers, we turn our heads
for fear of catching the fever. The weary limbs of weather's travels
fall. The wind says, *I did not mean to cause such harm,*
it was the rain that forced my hand. And the rain repents,
Those poor pretty flowers were such darlings.
I should not have drowned them.

In the wake of this new morning, the littered leaves and broken bulbs
are swept, water drains back to the river's mouth. The fine regret
of nights of misplaced passion, cold aggression, appears along the
orchard path. Groggy heads and aching temples bend the body down.
Is it true what happened? I must have succumbed to another voice.
I must have blacked out.

Somewhere, deep in the core of earth, a single believer signs
the season's petition. Winter's snow offers a clean white slate promise
of a second chance. And we make clear marks of our intentions
with sheltered feet, forgetful for a moment of summer's bones
struggling to stab the calm surface:
Alright, prove to me this time you mean business.

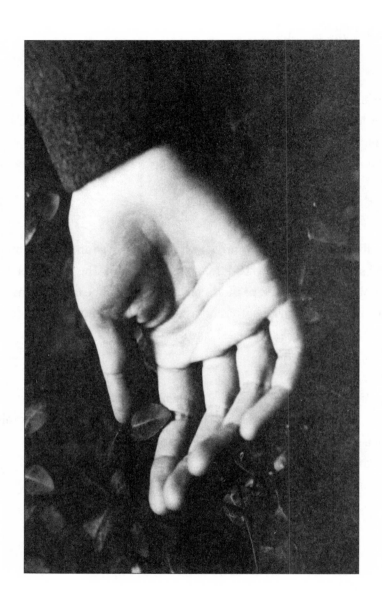

Foretelling God

I sing the progress of a deathless soul,
Whom Fate, which God made, but doth not control,
Placed in most shapes.

JOHN DONNE

Rain Season

The worst rain
since Noah's flood
a newscaster jokes

and we are locked inside
for the fourth day in a row
putting pans down.

The weeds on the lawn
have become greedy,
rise like trees

laugh at our attempts
to run by in plastic coats
and boots. On the highway

this morning
trout from the river
lay all over the roads

like ancient omens,
bodies cold against
the gravel, the stink

ungodly. There hasn't been
lightning like this in
forty years, my father tells me

over the phone
then tells me to get off
because it isn't safe. And remember

never to lift your finger
during a storm. You'll become
a conductor.

My love and I
out on the porch, getting soaked
despite the awning

kiss tentatively, where the drops
are strong and bloated
with death. In this city

we can be baptized by
the season but we can't
drink the water.

Entre Nous

Between you and me I had often envied Death
her thick black hair fanning
tight hands waving oblivious to cold
coveted the ability to force herself in anyone's company
sure of acceptance. I made my bed
and stopped breathing, fed the wet earth,
begged her to be my bride. And
while I slept, she cried against my side,
heavy with regret. Death
so easy to forget you, I steal back my hand
and while the dark wet handprint fades
watch how the depth of this hole
grows wide

Fear Falls Asleep on Duty

You can't blame him. Put yourself
in his tight shoes, his glasses framed to mimic
night. The hours are long and mostly dark
in his building. You must take note
of the slightest strange occurrence; keep
your eyes simultaneously on monitor
and elevator. Treat letters like ticking clocks.
Hold the phone to your ear like a grenade.

There is little chance for error. The windows
do not open and the stairs are not to be used
even in an emergency. That sweet old lady
for whom you hold the door every day has found
a weakness and tricked you, slipped a pill
into your coffee, is stealing
your edge as we speak.

Five Short Poems for Your Amusement at the Hospital

I

Manage your room like a hotel.
Phone down for food
and flowers. Be conspicuous
about guests.

Steal the robes.

II

Think of the things you've chased:
your brother when he was small
and used to pinch your cheeks, the moon,
the cat next door in the garden,
streetlights when they turn too fast, the rain,
fire, bureaucrats, all kinds of balls, lovers,
the express bus, shame, your mother's
memory.

Think that the world must now
come to you.

III

The kidneys are outrageous organs
greedy and unkind
they unwind
by punching people
in the ribs.

Who wants to make peace
with them anyway?

IV

The nurse and doctor have been
having an affair
for the last month

hot for each other
they run their hands on your belly
burning up

and you are the embers
keeping romance alive.

V

When they insist on taking more blood
and x-rays
pretend you are a prehistoric mammal
they are laying bare
to read your bones
uncover how you managed to survive
all this time.

Narcissus Becomes Hero

I'd say *Truth is Beauty* but I can't. There are millions
gathered along lakes and rivers, mirrored ceilings,
dazzled by their reflections, each one trying to outdo
the other, playing how far can you lean in—their pricks

held like lances against the water, not penetrating, merely floating…
Morpheus committed suicide. Helen has been hung.
Poor Leda raped herself, and Cupid, busy washing his chest,

hasn't noticed no one's actually *touching* thigh,
breast, calf, cock anymore. The picture-perfect are
kept at a distance and wrapped in plastic, eyes all

aflutter with the *thought* of who's applauding. Down
at the river's end, the waters rush for cover. The city's on fire
and not one hero can spare a moment, risk a bruise
on a pretty face for all the glory of the descending age.

Body Cast

The solution is simple:
Remake yourself. Fold your skin

like a warm blanket
cradle your sores
press your heart back in place.

Think of it as your wedding day.
Recall the rhythms of dance.
Construct a veil of white. Hold

on to your hurt like a forgiven friend.

Learn how to make each move count,
how to ask without speaking.

Embrace accidents—the debris
of what you were.

Fractures are a reliable cure.
Break your bones,
force them back together.

Afternoon Window Washer

While he naps I slip off the sheets
dip my gloves into the pail
and start to work.

I strip off his clothes and dump them
in the hamper.

Scrub his skin until it's white
clean of birthmarks
and freckles, erased of moles.
Hair falls like dead grass
collected in my hands.

If he wakes he knows to keep silent
and still. I have a job to do
and will not stop until everything is
spotless.

Pupils recede and his chest
becomes hard as an ironing board.

Then with bare fingernails I get
at the dirt in tough places: the bellybutton
and armpits. Between eyelashes.
I file his toes, until he is

perfectly clear and I can
see straight through him into
his neighbour's backyard.

Da Vinci's Notebook

reverse, she was
the canvas, her
symmetry
suspect in the light,
she moved
when the
darkness   grabbed
her like   a hand
and said, you
have it all wrong
Leo, I am   not an
offering or a sacrifice,
but a piece of glass.
Look for me in the
light. Red, in

Niagara Mermaids

A colony of nudists sing through the waves
loose like sheer capes
at the border of here and south,
quivering unabashedly in orgasm.

It's not the pirates or daredevils they want
or the hair of widows on balconies
stuck in their tracks with hearts spun like old records
under a mournful sun.

The honeymooners are who they desire
brimming with foam and white white sheets
trailing along the guardrail pungent with sex
even after a shower, still full of nerve.

Cascading down the cliff they signal,
follow the jump in their ears;
the mermaid voices sweeter, more difficult to cast
away than the lines of wedding bells.

The Car Thief

I begin with the trunk, prop
its lid open. Find
out if you're the type
to keep a spare tire, a booster cable,
bottles of antifreeze

or the kind who requires a mess
to keep moving
old candy wrappers, dirty sneakers,
lipstick tubes
and newspapers

ascertain whether
you are married or single by the small
items in your glove box
if you are childless
by the state of the mats.

I pull the steering wheel
to my lips,
feel if the seats are warm.

No question, it's an addiction.
I'm positive I could have fallen
for the woman who kept a map
of Italy on her dashboard.

No question.

For John Donne

You would have been my perfect lover:
a reckless man who shook the bed
and the pulpit, bled like a god
with three souls across continents.

Only you could strike the chord
of disbelief with a faith that never
faltered. Stand with feet firm, eyes
wide, a sorely battered heart.

You put your money where your
mouth was. Invited all to dwell
on your island. Cried: *This world
is the world I do love.*

Minister, you sung, and if no one
answered you sung louder.
You carved crosses into flutes
and drums. Ghosts into hosts.

But mostly, I admit, I know
I love you because in your elegies
no one dies. Women climb your bed
without fear or trembling, while across
our blessed hearts, a bell tolls *for thee.*

The Art of Breaking Wings

One must be careless
Love beauty in the abstract
Hold symmetry to be the most
Developed care of a soul

One must have affinities for angels
The real kind grounded in graveyards
Tips of loose wings
Hovering over their holes

Sleep in inappropriate places
Put yourself in someone's way
Tell your lover no matter what
He could never possibly hurt you

When it is time
Acknowledge yourself in a mirror
Make peace with order
Take off

Last Will and Testament

If my life is to be short (though whose is not?)
there are a few things you need to know:

I loved you unconditionally.

My favourite time was daybreak.

Between earth and sky I wanted
to be seen.

Not a day went by that I didn't mourn.

Watching you sleep was a secret passion.

Behind the dresser is some money.
Enough to take a trip.

I haunted ghosts and not the other away around.

My childlessness pleased me.

I was happy. You could say I was.

The things I forgot to say, I never would.
And the ones that hurt you, I still mean.

Don't forget the world is beautiful,
beautiful, my sweet, without me.

I never thought it would last.

I loved you all conditionally
until the end.

Foretelling God

In the beginning, before this world was created, God was created by a young man on his way to the hospital. He had an itch in his throat that couldn't be reached and a pain in his side doubled him over. Still, he insisted on walking to Emergency so he could stop in the park, smell the flowers and wave to his favourite counter girl at the coffee shop. There his dog lay waiting, paws tucked tenderly under his chin.

At the door he fainted and the nurses all screamed. Declared, "He must go to surgery, right away." "What will they do?" he cried. "Cut out the place that hurts," they replied. "Won't I miss it?" "No, it is nothing. Nothing." "Then don't bother to save it for me," the young man vowed. "Shove the stone in a jar and call it God." "Count to seven," the anesthetist told him, "and it will soon be over."

Acknowledgements and Dedications

This book wouldn't have been possible without the support and encouragement of three wonderful men: Barry Callaghan, my sardonic friend; Richard Teleky, my mentor and careful reader; and writer Christopher Doda, my companion and love.

I'd also like to thank everyone at Exile Editions for working with me once again, including Michael Callaghan for the painting, John Reeves, Tim Hanna for his inventive design & hard work, and Tracy Carbert who provided the cover art & interior images.

As well as for those listed above, many of the poems were written either directly or indirectly for the following people: my sister-in-law, Beryl Tennant (R.I.P.), for whom most of the poems from "Because a Body Drowns" are in tribute; my father, Avtar; my godmother, Gabrielle; all family and friends, especially shannon bramer and Annie & David Layton; and for all those people in this city and elsewhere who remind me why I do this in the first place: the old men and the little girls.

Lastly, I'd like to thank the editors of the following publications for publishing some of these poems in their previous incarnations: *Descant, Exile, The Literary Review of Canada, The New Canadian Poetry Anthology, Prairie Fire* and *Word Magazine*, in which "If Abraham" was awarded first prize in their first annual poetry competition; as well as composer Robert Baker and the ToneART ensemble for seeking me out and setting "Pretending to Die" to music."